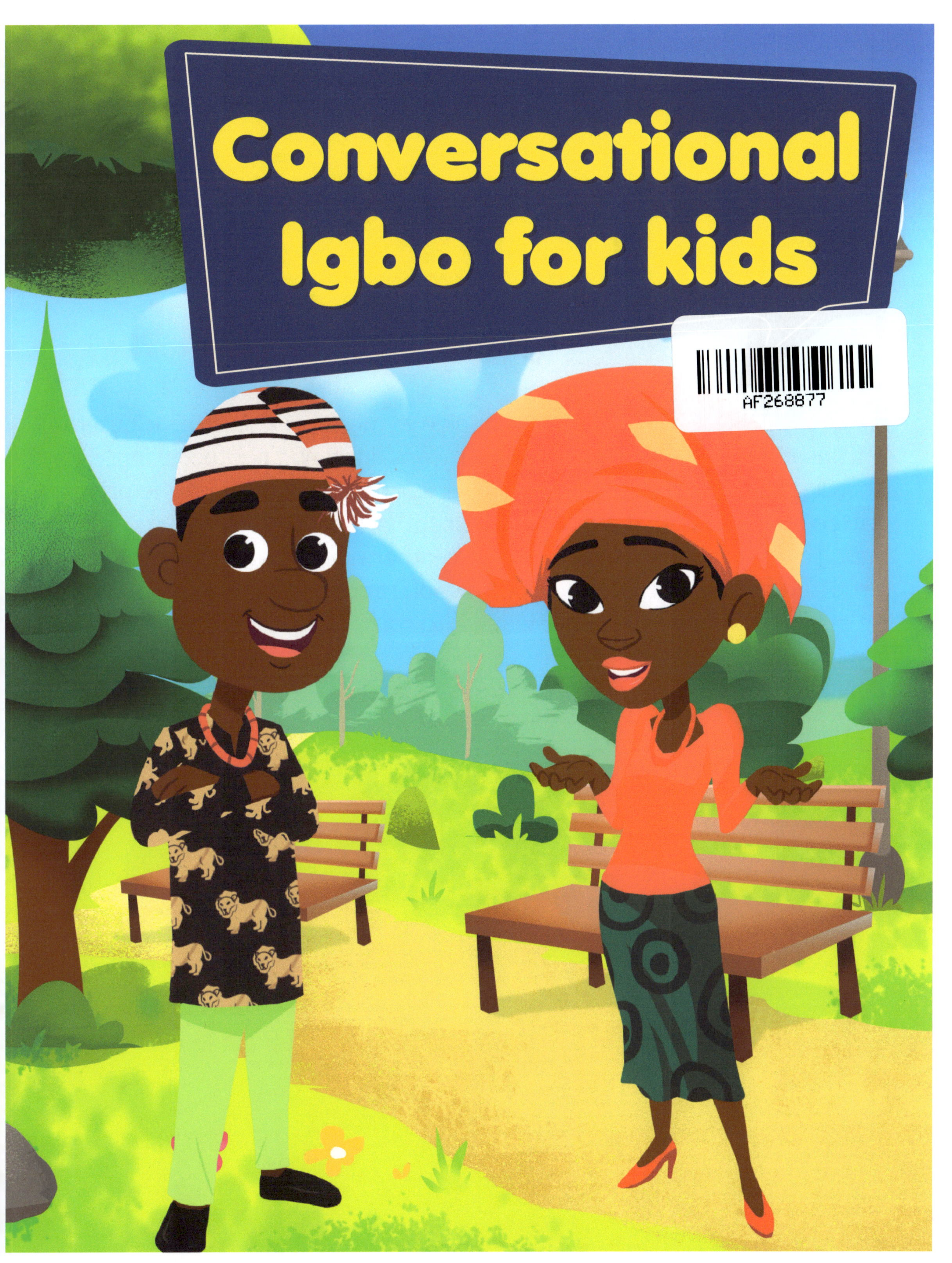

Conversational
Igbo for kids
AF268877

ISBN 978-1-8384397-0-5

WELCOME

Conversational Igbo for kids helps you learn to converse in Igbo using real-life situations. It covers situations like introductions, shopping, emergencies, moods, etc., with illustrated scenes to make learning Igbo easy and fun for beginners.

It comes with downloadable audio files (https://bit.ly/igbobookaudio), so you can listen to the conversations as you read. The book can also serve as a complementary guide to the Igbo102 module in the Genii Games App (https://geniigames.app). I hope you enjoy its simplicity, learn and showcase your growing conversational Igbo skills.

For corrections, suggestions, or contributions, please email hello@wafunkltd.com.

Thank you to:

Florence Onwuka, Patrick Diabuah (Voice and Content), Segun Samson (Illustrations), Tughu Aiyewa (Design), Chinwe Ononuju (Proofreading), Samuel Suraphel, Olatoro and Funke Adegbembo, CCHub Nigeria for your contributions, support, and motivation.

Imeela!

Adebayo Adegbembo

HOW TO USE THIS BOOK

The chapters are independent of one another. Hence, the reader can jump into any topic of choice.

Each chapter has reference audio files which you can download from https://bit.ly/igbobookaudio. The files are named to coincide with the Chapters. With those, you can listen to the sounds for actual pronunciations.

Follow the lessons carefully to understand the situation and sentences used.

The conversations flow from top to bottom in each panel. Read the topmost speech bubble first.

Igbo sentences are in Black texts and English translations in Blue texts.

Each chapter includes matching audio files to help the reader with the pronunciations.

Use the activities after lessons to test your skills. Check the answers towards the end of the book.

Table of Content

Part 1
Building Blocks

Ngozi describes herself and others in the first, second and third persons with examples. 🔊 Chapter 1

M / Mụ — Me

Mụ na gị.	Me and you.
Abụ m Chiọma.	I am Chiọma.
Aha m bụ Chiọma.	My name is Chiọma.

O / Ọ — He / She

Ọ bụ Chinaka.	She is Chinaka.
O nwere akpa.	He has a bag.

I / Ị — You (Singular)

Ị bụ Maazị Okeke.	You are Mr Okeke.
I nwere ego.	You have money.

Gị

Kedu ka di gị mere?
Ụlọ gị mara mma.
Mụ ma ọ bụ onye-nkuzi gị.
Mụ na onye-nkuzi gị.

You / Your

How is your husband?
Your house is beautiful.
Me or your teacher.
Me and your teacher.

Ya

Ọ bụ nke ya.
Ihe ya.
Nne ya gara ahịa.

His / Hers

It is his/her own.
His thing.
Her mother went to the market.

Anyị

Anyị dị mma.
Anyị na-abịa.

We / Us

We are fine.
We are coming.

Ha

Ha dị mma.
Ha na-eri nri.
Ha na-aga n'ụlọ akwụkwọ.

They / Them

They are fine.
They are eating.
They are going to school.

M   **Mine (Singular)**

Ọ bụ nke m.   It is mine.
Mma a bụ nke m.   This knife is mine.
Mma ahụ bụ nke m.   That knife is mine.

Anyi   **Ours (Plural)**

Ọ bụ nke anyị.   It is ours.

Gị   **Yours (Singular)**

Ọ bụ nke gị.   It is yours.
Akpa a bụ nke gị.   This bag is yours.
Asambodo ahụ bụ nke gị.   That certificate is yours.

Ha   **Theirs (Plural)**

Ọ bụ nke ha.   It is theirs.

Ngọzi is curious. She asks why, what, when, where and who with examples.   Chapter 2

Gịnị?   **What?**

Gịnị bụ nke a?	What is this?
Gịnị bụ nke ahụ?	What is that?
Gịnị bụ aha gị?	What is your name?
Gịnị ka ị chọrọ?	What do you want?

Onye?   **Who?**

Onye bụ nke a?	Who is this?
Onye bụ nke ahụ?	Who is that?
Onye ka ị bụ?	Who are you?
Onye na-akpọ m?	Who is calling me?

Ebee?

Ebee ka ị na-aga?	**Where are you going?**
Ebee ka i bi?	**Where do you live?**
Ebee ka ị nọ?	**Where are you?**
Ebee ka i si?	**Where are you from?**

Where?

Kedu mgbe?

Kedu mgbe ị na-aga?	**When are you going?**
Kedu mgbe ị na-abia?	**When are you coming?**
Kedu mgbe ị bịara?	**When did you arrive?**
Kedu mgbe ị ga-alọta?	**When will you return?**
Kedu mgbe mmemme ahụ bidoro?	**When did the event start?**
Kedu mgbe mmemme a ga-ebido?	**When will the event start?**

When?

Gịnị?

Gịnị mere na ị biaghị n'oge?	**Why are you late?**
Gịnị ka ị na-akpọrọ m?	**Why are you calling me?**

Why?

1. How do you say, 'WHAT is this?'

2. How do you say, 'WHAT is that?'

3. To ask someone WHAT his or her name is:

4. To ask someone WHAT he or she wants:

5. How do you say, 'WHO is this?'

6. How do you say, 'WHO is that?'

7. How do you say, 'WHO are you?'

8. How do you say, 'WHO is calling me?'

9. To ask WHERE someone is going:

10. To ask WHERE someone lives:

11. To ask someone WHERE he or she is:

12. To find out WHERE someone is from:

13. To ask WHY someone is calling you:

14. To ask WHY someone is late:

15. To ask WHEN someone is going somewhere:

16. To ask WHEN someone is coming to see you:

17. To ask someone WHEN he or she arrived:

18. To find out WHEN someone will return from a trip:

Part 2
Conversations

Lesson 3 Introductions

Obinna and Ngọzi meet for the first time. They learn each other's names, professions and more. Chapter 3

Ebi m na Awka.
I live in Awka.
Ebee ka i bi?
Where do you live?
Imeela.
Thank you.
Obi di m utọ ihu gi.
Nice to meet you.
Ka ọ di.
See you soon.
Ka emesia.
Goodbye.

Check the answers on page 55

1. To say, 'how are you?':
2. To respond to a hello greeting by saying, 'you are fine?':
3. To ask someone for his or her name:
4. To tell someone your name is Ngọzi:
5. To ask someone where he or she is from:
6. To tell someone you are from Enugu:
7. To ask a friend for his or her age:
8. To ask a friend for his or her profession:
9. To tell someone you are a teacher:
10. To ask someone where he or she lives:
11. To tell someone you live in Awka:
12. To express your pleasure after meeting someone:
13. To say goodbye to someone:
14. To tell a friend you are 10 years old:
15. To tell a friend you will see him or her soon:

Ngọzi gains more understanding of Igbo by asking Obinna to repeat certain words.   Chapter 4

Kedu ka ị ga-esi kwuo English n'Igbo?
How do you say English in Igbo?
Bekee.
English.

Kedu ihe a na-akpọ English n'Igbo?
What is English called in Igbo?
Bekee.
English.

Ị ghọtara ya?
Do you understand?
Mba. Aghọtaghi m.
No. I don't understand.

Biko, na-asụ nwayọọ nwayọọ.
Please, speak slowly.
Bekee.
English.

Biko, kwugharịa ya.
Please, repeat it.
Bekee.
English.

Ị ghọtara ya?
Do you understand?
Ee. Aghọtara m. Imeela.
Yes. I understand. Thank you.

Check the answers on page 56

1. To greet a friend casually:

2. To respond to a casual hello greeting:

3. To tell someone you have some questions to ask:

4. To tell someone you are listening to him or her:

5. To ask someone if he or she speaks Igbo:

6. To tell someone you speak a bit of Igbo:

7. To tell someone you speak Igbo very well:

8. To ask for the translation of English in Igbo:

9. To ask if someone understands something:

10. To tell someone you do not understand something:

11. To tell someone to repeat a statement:

12. To tell someone you understand something:

13. To say thank you to a friend:

14. To tell someone you will see him or her later:

15. To tell someone you do not speak Igbo very well:

16. To tell someone to speak slowly:

17. What do you call English in Igbo?

18. How do you say, 'And you?' or 'What about you?'

Lesson 5 Shopping

Obinna is in the market to buy vegetables. He asks for a certain quantity and bargains with the seller. Chapter 5

Kedu nke ị chọrọ?
Which one do you want?
Achọrọ m nke a.
I want this.

Ego ole ka ọ bụ?
How much is it?
Naịra atọ.
Three Naira.

Ọ dị ọnụ.
It is too expensive.
Ọ dịghị ọnụ.
It is not expensive.

Ka m kwụọ otu naịra.
Let me pay 1 Naira.
Mba. Ekweghị m.
No. I disagree.

Ole bụ ọnụ ikpeazu ya?
What is the last price?
Naịra abụọ na kọbọ iri ise.
2 Naira 50 kobo.

Aga m akwu naịra abụọ.
I'll pay 2 Naira.
Anụla m.
I have heard.
I kwere?
Do you agree?
Ee. Kwuo.
Yes. Pay.
Were.
Take.
Imeela.
Thank you.
Ọgwụla ihe i chọrọ?
Is that all you want?
Ee. Ọ gwụla.
Yes. That's all.
Ahịa ọma.
I wish you good sales.
Imeela. Ka emesia.
Thank you. Goodbye.

Check the answers on page 57

1. To ask if someone sells vegetables:

2. To respond, Yes, to a question:

3. To tell a seller you want to view some items before buying:

4. To ask how many items someone wants:

5. To tell a seller you want two items:

6. To tell a seller to give you another item:

7. To ask if a buyer has finished shopping:

8. To ask how much an item costs:

9. To tell a seller an item is too expensive:

10. To bargain for a lower price:

11. To confirm if a seller agrees to your price:

12. To tell someone you don't agree to a price:

13. To wish a seller good sales after shopping:

14. To ask someone what he or she wants:

15. If something costs 3 Naira, you can say:

16. To tell a seller you want an item you're pointing at:

17. To say something is not expensive:

Lesson 6 — Dining

Ngozi is hungry. In the restaurant, she and Obinna interact with the seller for food and more. **Chapter 6**

Ego ole ka ọ pụtara?
How much is the total sum?
Naịra iri na otu.
11 Naira.
Were ego gi.
Take your money.
Imeela.
Thank you.
Bia rie nri.
Come and eat.
Imeela.
Thank you.
Kedu ka nri a di?
How is the food?
Ọ di uto.
It is delicious.
Kedu ka ofe a di?
How is the soup?
Ose kariri.
It is spicy.
Biko, nye m mmiri.
Please, give me water.
Were.
Take.
Wetere m mma.
Bring me a knife.
Ana m ewete ya.
I am bringing it.

Achoro m nnu.
I need salt.
Lee ya.
Here it is.

I ka choro nri?
Do you want more food?
Mba. Afọ ejula m.
No. I am full.

Afọ ejubeghi m.
I'm not full.
Gị kwanụ?
And you?

M chọkwara osikapa ọzo.
I want more rice.
Obere ka ọ bu nnukwu?
Small or large quantity?

Obere.
A little.
Anụla m.
I have heard.

Imeela.
Thank you.
Were.
Take.

Check the answers on page 58

1. To tell someone you are hungry:

2. To ask what someone wants to eat:

3. To tell someone you want to eat rice and beans:

4. To ask if rice and beans are available:

5. To tell someone to give you rice and beans:

6. To ask how much a plate of food costs:

7. To ask how much an item costs:

8. When paying for a service, you can say:

9. To ask what someone thinks of the food he is eating:

10. To tell someone the food you are eating is delicious:

11. To tell someone the food you are eating is spicy:

12. To tell someone you want salt:

13. To tell someone you want more rice:

14. After eating, to tell someone 'you are full':

15. After eating, to tell someone 'you are not full':

16. If you want a small quantity between two options, you can say:

17. To invite someone to go off to eat with you:

18. When passing an item to someone, you can say:

19. To ask if someone wants more food:

20. To tell someone to give you five pieces of meat:

21. To ask if a specific item (goat meat) is available:

22. To ask for the total cost of a service or goods:

Ngozi and Obinna are at a bar to have some drinks. They interact with the seller for drinks and more. 🔊 **Chapter 7**

Ọ gwụla.
That's all.
Kedu ihe ọzọ ị chọrọ?
What else do you want?
Ego ole ka ọ bụ?
How much is it?
Otu naịra.
1 Naira.
Were.
Take.
Imeela.
Thank you.

Check the answers on page 59

1. To tell someone you are thirsty:
2. To ask if drinks are available:
3. To ask someone what he or she wants to drink:
4. To tell someone you have water and other drinks, you can say:
5. To tell someone to give you water:
6. To ask if someone wants something else:
7. To tell someone to give you cold water, you can say:
8. To ask how much a drink costs:
9. When passing something to someone, you can say:
10. To tell someone, that's all, you can say:
11. To express gratitude when given a drink:
12. To tell someone you have all sorts of an item, you can say:

Lesson 8 — Commuting

Ngọzi wants to make a short trip across town. She finds a taxi, describes her destination to the driver and more. Chapter 8

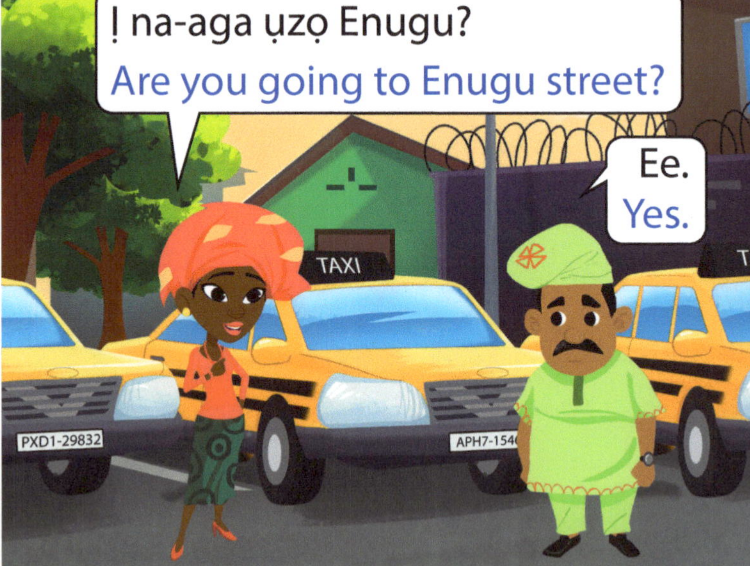

Biko, banye.
Please, enter.
Ngwanụ.
Alright.
Anụla m.
I've heard.
Biko, kwụsị ebe a.
Please, stop here.
Imeela.
Thank you.
Were ego gị.
Take your money.
Ka emesia.
Goodbye.
Ka emesia.
Goodbye.

Check the answers on page 60

1. To greet a taxi driver at work, you can say:

2. To ask a taxi driver for his or her destination:

3. To ask for the taxi fare:

4. To ask if a taxi driver is going to a specific destination (Enugu):

5. If a driver asks if you are going to a destination and you are not, say:

6. To tell someone to enter a vehicle:

7. To tell a taxi driver you want to stop somewhere:

8. When paying the taxi driver, you can say:

9. If a driver asks if you are going to a destination and you are, say:

10. To tell someone goodbye:

Ngọzi wants to travel out of town. She and Obinna discuss her destination, time of departure and more. 🔊 Chapter 9

Izu uka na-abịa.
Next week.

Kedu mgbe ị ga-alọta?
When will you return?

Ị na-aga naanị gị?
Are you going alone?

Mba. Mụ na ezi na ụlọ m.
No. With my family.

Kedu mgbe ị ga-apụ?
What time will you leave?

Elekere abụọ nke ehihie.
2 P.M.

Imeela. Ka emesia.
Thank you. Goodbye.

Ije ọma.
Safe journey.

Check the answers on page 61

1. To inform a friend that you are about to travel:

2. To ask where someone is travelling to:

3. To ask when someone is travelling:

4. To respond to someone that you are travelling tomorrow, you can say:

5. To ask when someone will return from a trip:

6. To ask for the exact time someone will travel:

7. To tell someone you are travelling at 2 PM, you can say:

8. To tell someone goodbye:

9. To ask if someone is travelling alone:

10. To tell someone you are travelling with your family, you can say:

11. To tell someone you are travelling next week, you can say:

12. To tell someone you are travelling to Anambra:

13. To tell someone you have heard him or her:

14. To wish someone a safe journey:

Lesson 10 Directions

Ngozi needs help getting to the market. She gets directions from Obinna who is familiar with the route. Chapter 10

Biko, dee ya.
Please write it down.
Oo.
Alright.
Biko, kwugharịa ya.
Please, repeat it.
Anụla m.
I've heard.
Na-aga.
Keep walking.
Ngwanụ.
Alright.
N'akụkụ, gafee ụzọ.
By the corner, cross the road.
Ngwanụ.
Alright.
Gaa aka nri. Tụgharịa aka-ekpe.
Walk towards the right. Turn left.
Aghọtara m.
I understand.
Kedu ụzọ mbata?
Where is the entrance?
Ebe a.
Here.
Kedu ụzọ ọpụpụ?
Where is the exit?
Ebe ahụ.
Over there.

Check the answers on page 62

1. To tell someone to direct you somewhere:

2. To ask where somewhere (market) is:

3. To ask if somewhere is faraway:

4. To ask if somewhere is nearby:

5. To tell someone her destination is a 5-minutes-walk, you can say:

6. To tell someone to turn left:

7. To tell someone to turn or go right:

8. To tell someone to repeat a direction, you can say:

9. To ask for the entrance, you can say:

10. To ask for the exit, you can say:

11. To tell someone her destination is 'right here', you can say:

12. To tell someone her destination is 'over there', you can say:

13. To tell someone to write something down:

14. To tell someone his or her destination is not faraway:

15. To ask how to get to a destination (market):

16. To tell someone you understand something:

17. To tell someone to cross the road:

Lesson 11 Moods

Ngọzi is having mood swings. Obinna asks how she's feeling and she expresses her moods to him. 🔊 **Chapter 11**

Kedu ka i mere?
How are you?
Obi adịghị m ụtọ.
I am sad.
Biko, gawa.
Please go away.
Gịnị mere?
What is it?
Ụjọ na-atụ m.
I am scared.
Emetula m aka.
Don't touch me.
Gịnị mere?
What is it?
Ahụ na-afụ m ụfụ.
I am pained.
Hapụ m aka.
Leave me alone.

Gịnị mere?
What is it?
Ọ tụrụ m n'anya.
I am surprised.
Atụrụla m asị.
Don't lie to me.
Kedu ka i mere?
How are you?
Obi dị m ụtọ.
I am excited.
Gwa m eziokwu.
Tell me the truth.
Ahụrụ m gị n'anya.
I love you.
Ahụrụ m gị n'anya.
I love you.
Imeela.
Thank you.

Check the answers on page 63

1. To ask how someone is feeling:

2. To tell someone you are angry:

3. To tell someone you are excited or happy:

4. To tell someone you are sad:

5. To tell someone you want to be left alone:

6. To tell someone to 'go away':

7. To ask someone why he or she feels someway, you can say:

8. To tell someone you are scared:

9. To tell someone to say the truth:

10. To tell someone not to tell you lies:

11. To tell someone you are surprised:

12. To tell someone you are pained, say:

13. To tell someone you love him or her:

14. To tell someone you are feeling sleepy:

15. When you do not want someone to touch you, say:

16. When you do not want someone to offend you, say:

17. To tell someone you are tired:

Lesson 12 Emergencies

Ngọzi experiences various emergencies. She calls for help and explains her situation. Chapter 12

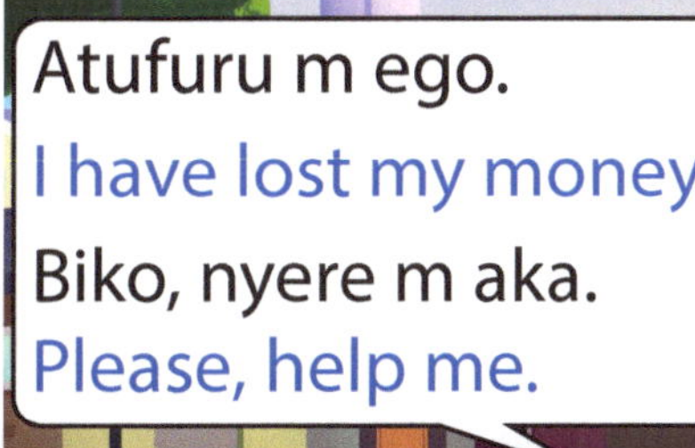

Nyere anyị aka!
Help us!
Gịnị mere?
What is the matter?

Ezuru anyị ohi.
We have just been robbed.
Biko, kpọọ ndị uweojii.
Please, call the police.

Nyere m aka!
Help me!
Gịnị mere?
What is the matter?

Enwere m ihe mberede.
I had an accident.
Achọrọ m dọkịta.
I need a doctor.

Nyere m aka!
Help me!
Gịnị mere?
What is it?

Isi na-awa m.
I have a headache.
Achọrọ m dọkịta.
I need a doctor.

Nyere m aka!
Help me!
Gịnị mere?
What is it?

Ahụ na-afụ m ụfụ.
My body aches.
Achọrọ m dọkịta.
I need a doctor.

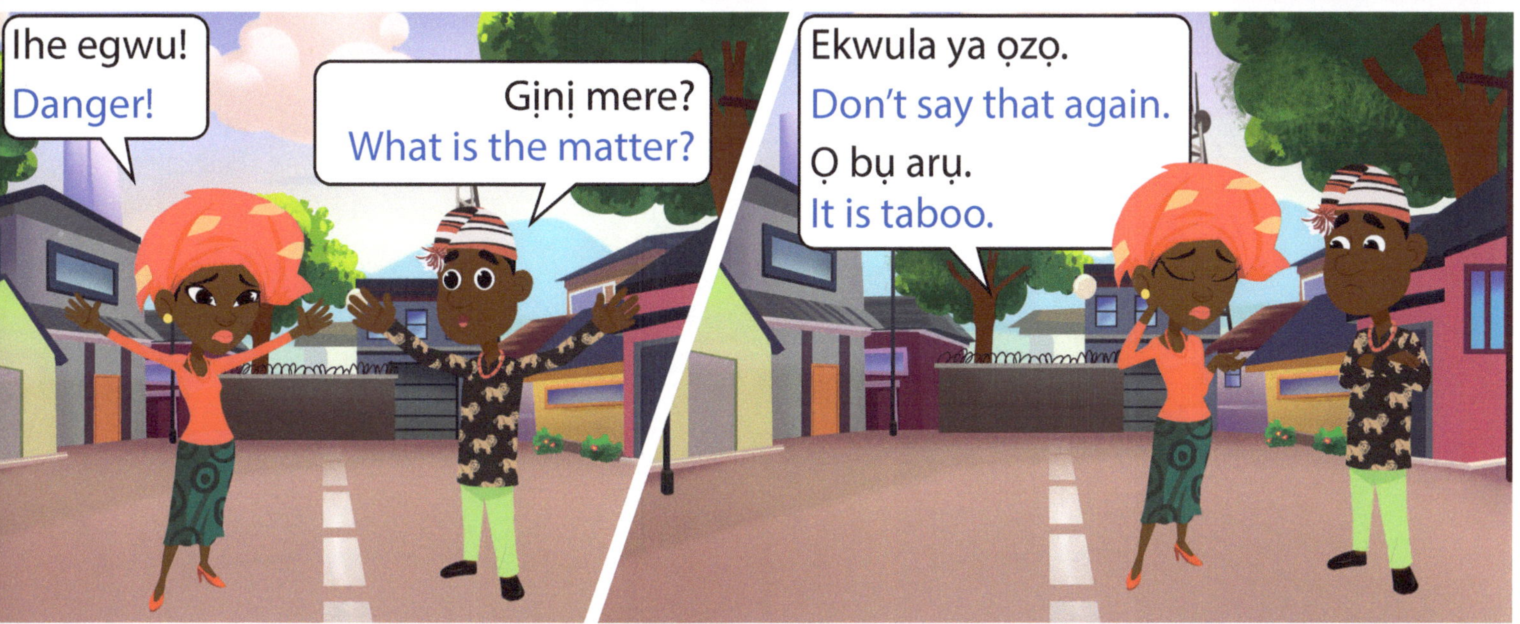

Ihe egwu!
Danger!
Gịnị mere?
What is the matter?
Ekwula ya ọzọ.
Don't say that again.
Ọ bụ arụ.
It is taboo.

Nyere m aka!
Help me!
Gịnị mere?
What is the matter?

Agbajiri m ụkwụ.
I broke my leg.
Achọrọ m dọkịta.
I need a doctor.

Nyere m aka! Bia ọsọ ọsọ.
Help me! Come quickly.
Gịnị mere?
What is it?

Nsogbu adịghị.
No problem.
Ndo.
Sorry.

Biko! Kedu ụlọ mpochi?
Please! Where is the toilet?
Gịnị mere?
What is the matter?

Achọrọ m ịnyụ amịrị.
I want to pee.
Ebee ka m ga-anyụ amịrị.
Where can I pee?

Biko! Kedu ụlọ mpochi?
Please! Where is the toilet?
Gịnị mere?
What is the matter?

Achọrọ m ịnyụ nsị.
I want to poo.
Ebee ka m ga-anyụ nsị.
Where can I poo?

Check the answers on page 64

1. To call for help when you are in danger:
2. To ask about a situation:
3. To tell someone you have missed your way:
4. To call for help when you and another person are in danger, say:
5. To tell someone you have lost your money:
6. To tell someone there is a fire:
7. To tell someone to call the police:
8. To say 'sorry' to someone:
9. To tell someone you need to see a doctor:
10. To tell someone something is taboo:
11. To tell someone not to say something again:
12. To tell someone you had an accident:
13. To tell someone you have a headache:
14. To tell someone your body aches:
15. To tell someone to come urgently:
16. To ask where the toilet is:
17. To tell someone you want to poo:
18. To tell someone you want to pee:
19. To tell someone you have broken your leg:
20. To warn someone of danger:

Lesson 13 Catching up

Ngọzi and Obinna catch up after a while. They talk about different people, events and more. Chapter 13

I chetere Uchenna?
Do you remember Uchenna?
Ee. Kelee ha.
Yes. Extend my regards.
Ị maara Chukwudi?
Do you know Chukwudi?
Mba. Amaghị m Chukwudi.
No. I don't know Chukwudi.
Ebee ka Chioma nọ?
Where is Chioma?
Ọ nọ Onitsha.
She is in Onitsha.
Ị maara Obinna?
Do you know Obinna?
Ee. Amataara m Obinna.
Yes. I know Obinna.
Kedu ka o mere?
How is he?
Ọ dị mma.
He is fine.
Ị nụrụ maka Obiora?
Did you hear about Obiora?
Ee.
Yes.

Ị ma maka mmeme ahụ?
Did you know about the event?
Ee.
Yes.
Ị gụrụ maka akụkọ ahụ?
Did you read about that story?
Obere.
Partly.
Kelee onye ọbụla.
Extend my regards to everyone.
Ka ọ dị oge ọzọ.
I have to go now.
Anụla m.
I have heard.
Kelee Ugonna.
Extend my greetings to Ugonna.

Check the answers on page 65

1. To say hello to a friend:

2. To respond to a hello greeting, you can say:

3. When you are just seeing someone after a long time, you can say:

4. To ask a friend where he or she is:

5. To tell someone you are at home:

6. To ask about someone's dad:

7. To ask about someone's household:

8. To ask a friend if he or she remembers Uchenna:

9. To ask if someone knows Chukwudi:

10. To tell someone you do not know Chukwudi:

11. To ask if someone knows about an event:

12. To tell someone 'you are about to go now':

13. To tell someone, Yes, you can say:

14. To ask for Chiọma's whereabout:

15. To respond that you know Obinna:

16. To ask if someone read about a story or news:

17. To tell someone you have heard him or her:

18. To tell someone you know a bit of something:

19. To ask a friend if he or she heard about Obiọra:

20. To tell someone, No, you can say:

21. To respond that another person is in Onitsha:

Answers

Question words Activity Page 12

1.	How do you say, 'WHAT is this?'	Gịnị bụ nke a?
2.	How do you say, 'WHAT is that?'	Gịnị bụ nke ahụ?
3.	To ask someone WHAT his or her name is:	Gịnị bụ aha gị?
4.	To ask someone WHAT he or she wants:	Gịnị ka ị chọrọ?
5.	How do you say, 'WHO is this?'	Onye bụ nke a?
6.	How do you say, 'WHO is that?'	Onye bụ nke ahụ?
7.	How do you say, 'WHO are you?'	Onye ka ị bụ?
8.	How do you say, 'WHO is calling me?'	Onye na-akpọ m?
9.	To ask WHERE someone is going:	Ebee ka ị na-aga?
10.	To ask WHERE someone lives:	Ebee ka i bi?
11.	To ask someone WHERE he or she is:	Ebee ka ị nọ?
12.	To find out WHERE someone is from:	Ebee ka i si?
13.	To ask WHY someone is calling you:	Gịnị ka ị na-akpọrọ m?
14.	To ask WHY someone is late:	Gịnị mere na ị biaghị n'oge?
15.	To ask WHEN someone is going somewhere:	Kedu mgbe ị na-aga?
16.	To ask WHEN someone is coming to see you:	Kedu mgbe ị na-abia?
17.	To ask someone WHEN he or she arrived:	Kedu mgbe ị biara?
18.	To find out WHEN someone will return from a trip:	Kedu mgbe ị ga-alọta?

Introductions Activity Page 16

1. To say, 'how are you?': — Kedu ka i mere?
2. To respond to a hello greeting by saying, 'you are fine?': — Adị m mma.
3. To ask someone for his or her name: — Gịnị bụ aha gi?
4. To tell someone your name is Ngọzi: — Aha m bụ Ngọzi.
5. To ask someone where he or she is from: — Ebee ka i si?
6. To tell someone you are from Enugu: — Esi m Enugu.
7. To ask a friend for his or her age: — Afọ ole ka ị dị?
8. To ask a friend for his or her profession: — Gịnị ka ị na-arụ?
9. To tell someone you are a teacher: — Abu m onye-nkuzi.
10. To ask someone where he or she lives: — Ebee ka i bi?
11. To tell someone you live in Awka: — Ebi m na Awka.
12. To express your pleasure after meeting someone: — Obi di m utọ ihu gi.
13. To say goodbye to someone: — Ka emesia.
14. To tell a friend you are 10 years old: — Adị m afọ iri.
15. To tell a friend you will see him or her soon: — Ka ọ di.

Understanding Activity Page 19

1. To greet a friend casually: Kedu kwanụ?

2. To respond to a casual hello greeting: Ọ dị mma.

3. To tell someone you have some questions to ask: Biko, enwere m ụfọdụ ajụjụ.

4. To tell someone you are listening to him or her: Ana m ege ntị.

5. To ask someone if he or she speaks Igbo: Ị na-asụ Igbo?

6. To tell someone you speak a bit of Igbo: Ana m asụ Igbo obere obere.

7. To tell someone you speak Igbo very well: Ana m asụ Igbo nke ọma.

8. To ask for the translation of English in Igbo: Kedu ihe a na-akpọ English n'Igbo?

9. To ask if someone understands something: Ị ghọtara ya?

10. To tell someone you do not understand something: Aghọtaghi m.

11. To tell someone to repeat a statement: Biko, kwugharịa ya.

12. To tell someone you understand something: Aghọtara m.

13. To say thank you to a friend: Imeela.

14. To tell someone you will see him or her later: Ka ọ dị.

15. To tell someone you do not speak Igbo very well: Anaghị m asụ Igbo nke ọma.

16. To tell someone to speak slowly: Na-asụ nwayọọ nwayọọ.

17. What do you call English in Igbo? Bekee.

18. How do you say, 'And you?' or 'What about you?' Gị onwe gị kwanụ?

Shopping Activity Page 23

#		
1.	To ask if someone sells vegetables:	Ị na-ere ahịhịa nri?
2.	To respond, Yes, to a question:	Ee.
3.	To tell a seller you want to view some items before buying:	Ka m hụ ha.
4.	To ask how many items someone wants:	Ole ka ị chọrọ?
5.	To tell a seller you want two items:	Achọrọ m abụọ.
6.	To tell a seller to give you another item:	Nye m ọzọ.
7.	To ask if a buyer has finished shopping:	Ọgwụla Ihe i chọrọ?
8.	To ask how much an item costs:	Ego ole ka ọ bụ?
9.	To tell a seller an item is too expensive:	Ọ dị ọnụ.
10.	To bargain for a lower price:	Ole bụ ọnụ ikpeazu ya?
11.	To confirm if a seller agrees to your price:	I kwere?
12.	To tell someone you don't agree to a price:	Mba. Ekweghị m.
13.	To wish a seller good sales after shopping:	Ahia ọma.
14.	To ask someone what he or she wants:	Kedu nke ị chọrọ?
15.	If something costs 3 Naira, you can say:	Naịra atọ.
16.	To tell a seller you want an item you're pointing at:	Achọrọ m nke a.
17.	To say something is not expensive:	Ọ dịghị ọnụ.

Dining Activity Page 27

1. To tell someone you are hungry: — Aguu na-agu m.
2. To ask what someone wants to eat: — Kedu ihe i choro iri?
3. To tell someone you want to eat rice and beans: — Achoro m iri osikapa na agwa.
4. To ask if rice and beans are available: — I nwere osikapa na agwa?
5. To tell someone to give you rice and beans: — Nye m osikapa na agwa.
6. To ask how much a plate of food costs: — Ego ole bu otu efere?
7. To ask how much an item costs: — Ego ole ka o bu?
8. When paying for a service, you can say: — Were ego gi.
9. To ask what someone thinks of the food he is eating: — Kedu ka nri a di?
10. To tell someone the food you are eating is delicious: — O di uto.
11. To tell someone the food you are eating is spicy: — Ose kariri.
12. To tell someone you want salt: — Achoro m nnu.
13. To tell someone you want more rice: — M chokwara osikapa ozo.
14. After eating, to tell someone 'you are full': — Afo ejula m.
15. After eating, to tell someone 'you are not full': — Afo ejubeghi m.
16. If you want a small quantity between two options, you can say: — Obere.
17. To invite someone to go off to eat with you: — Ka anyi gaa rie nri.
18. When passing an item to someone, you can say: — Were.
19. To ask if someone wants more food: — I ka choro nri?
20. To tell someone to give you five pieces of meat: — Nye m anu ise.
21. To ask if a specific item (goat meat) is available: — I nwere anu ewu?
22. To ask for the total cost of a service or goods: — Ego ole ka o putara?

Drinking Activity Page 30

1. To tell someone you are thirsty: — Achọrọ m ịṅụ mmanya.
2. To ask if drinks are available: — I nwere mmanya?
3. To ask someone what he or she wants to drink: — Kedu nke ị chọrọ ịṅụ?
4. To tell someone you have water and other drinks, you can say: — Anyị nwere mmiri, na ndị ọzọ.
5. To tell someone to give you water: — Nye m mmiri.
6. To ask if someone wants something else: — Kedu ihe ọzọ ị chọrọ?
7. To tell someone to give you cold water, you can say: — Mmiri oyi.
8. To ask how much a drink costs: — Ego ole ka ọ bụ?
9. When passing something to someone, you can say: — Were.
10. To tell someone, that's all, you can say: — Ọ gwụla.
11. To express gratitude when given a drink: — Imeela.
12. To tell someone you have all sorts of an item, you can say: — Anyị nwere ụdị dị iche iche.

Commuting Activity Page 33

1. To greet a taxi driver at work, you can say: Jisie ike.

2. To ask a taxi driver for his or her destination: Ebee ka ị na-aga?

3. To ask for the taxi fare: Ego ole?

4. To ask if a taxi driver is going to a specific Ị na-aga ụzọ Enugu?
   destination (Enugu):

5. If a driver asks if you are going to a destination and you are not, say: Mba.

6. To tell someone to enter a vehicle: Banye.

7. To tell a taxi driver you want to stop somewhere: Biko, kwụsị ebe a.

8. When paying the taxi driver, you can say: Were ego gị.

9. If a driver asks if you are going to a destination and you are, say: Ee.

10. To tell someone goodbye: Ka emesia.

Travelling Activity Page 36

1.	To inform a friend that you are about to travel:	Achọrọ m ime njem.
2.	To ask where someone is travelling to:	Kedu ebe ị na-aga?
3.	To ask when someone is travelling:	Kedu mgbe ị na-aga?
4.	To respond to someone that you are travelling tomorrow, you can say:	Echi.
5.	To ask when someone will return from a trip:	Kedu mgbe ị ga-alọta?
6.	To ask for the exact time someone will travel:	Kedu mgbe ị ga-apụ?
7.	To tell someone you are travelling at 2 PM, you can say:	Elekere abụọ nke ehihie.
8.	To tell someone goodbye:	Ka emesia.
9.	To ask if someone is travelling alone:	Ị na-aga naanị gị?
10.	To tell someone you are travelling with your family, you can say:	Mụ na ezi na ụlọ m.
11.	To tell someone you are travelling next week, you can say:	Izu uka na-abịa.
12.	To tell someone you are travelling to Anambra:	Ana m aga Anambra.
13.	To tell someone you have heard him or her:	Anụla m.
14.	To wish someone a safe journey:	Ije ọma.

Directions Activity Page 39

1.	To tell someone to direct you somewhere:	Biko, gosị m ụzọ.
2.	To ask where somewhere (market) is:	Kedu ebe ahịa dị?
3.	To ask if somewhere is faraway:	Ọ dị anya?
4.	To ask if somewhere is nearby:	Ọ dị nso?
5.	To tell someone her destination is a 5-minutes-walk, you can say:	Ije nkeji ise.
6.	To tell someone to turn left:	Tụgharịa aka-ekpe.
7.	To tell someone to turn or go right:	Gaa aka nri.
8.	To tell someone to repeat a direction, you can say:	Biko, kwugharịa ya.
9.	To ask for the entrance, you can say:	Kedu ụzọ mbata?
10.	To ask for the exit, you can say:	Kedu ụzọ ọpụpụ?
11.	To tell someone her destination is 'right here', you can say:	Ebe a.
12.	To tell someone her destination is 'over there', you can say:	Ebe ahụ.
13.	To tell someone to write something down:	Dee ya.
14.	To tell someone his or her destination is not faraway:	Ọ dịghị anya.
15.	To ask how to get to a destination (market):	Kedu ụzọ m ga-esi gaa ahịa?
16.	To tell someone you understand something:	Aghọtara m.
17.	To tell someone to cross the road:	Gafee ụzọ.

Moods Activity Page 43

1. To ask how someone is feeling: — Kedu ka i mere?
2. To tell someone you are angry: — Iwe na-ewe m.
3. To tell someone you are excited or happy: — Obi dị m ụtọ.
4. To tell someone you are sad: — Obi adịghị m ụtọ.
5. To tell someone you want to be left alone: — Hapụ m aka.
6. To tell someone to 'go away': — Biko, gawa.
7. To ask someone why he or she feels someway, you can say: — Ọ bụ gịnị mere?
8. To tell someone you are scared: — Ụjọ na-atụ m.
9. To tell someone to say the truth: — Gwa m eziokwu.
10. To tell someone not to tell you lies: — Atụrụla m asị.
11. To tell someone you are surprised: — Ọ tụrụ m n'anya.
12. To tell someone you are pained, say: — Ahụ na-afụ m ụfụ.
13. To tell someone you love him or her: — Ahụrụ m gị n'anya.
14. To tell someone you are feeling sleepy: — Achọrọ m ịrahụ ụra.
15. When you do not want someone to touch you, say: — Emetula m aka.
16. When you do not want someone to offend you, say: — Akpasula m iwe.
17. To tell someone you are tired: — Ike gwụrụ m.

Emergencies Activity Page 48

1.	To call for help when you are in danger:	Nyere m aka!
2.	To ask about a situation:	Gịnị mere?
3.	To tell someone you have missed your way:	Agafuru m ụzọ.
4.	To call for help when you and another person are in danger, say:	Nyere anyị aka!
5.	To tell someone you have lost your money:	Atufuru m ego.
6.	To tell someone there is a fire:	Ọkụ na-agba.
7.	To tell someone to call the police:	Biko, kpọọ ndị uweojii.
8.	To say 'sorry' to someone:	Ndo.
9.	To tell someone you need to see a doctor:	Achọrọ m dọkịta.
10.	To tell someone something is taboo:	Ọ bụ arụ.
11.	To tell someone not to say something again:	Ekwula ya ọzọ.
12.	To tell someone you had an accident:	Enwere m ihe mberede.
13.	To tell someone you have a headache:	Isi na-awa m.
14.	To tell someone your body aches:	Ahụ na-afụ m ụfụ.
15.	To tell someone to come urgently:	Bia ọsọ ọsọ.
16.	To ask where the toilet is:	Ebee ka m ga-anyụ nsị?
17.	To tell someone you want to poo:	Achọrọ m ịnyụ nsị.
18.	To tell someone you want to pee:	Achọrọ m ịnyụ amịrị.
19.	To tell someone you have broken your leg:	Agbajiri m ụkwụ.
20.	To warn someone of danger:	Ihe egwu!

Catching up Activity Page 52

1. To say hello to a friend: — Kedu ka i mere?
2. To respond to a hello greeting, you can say: — Adị m mma.
3. When you are just seeing someone after a long time, you can say: — Otekwala.
4. To ask a friend where he or she is: — Ebee ka i nọ?
5. To tell someone you are at home: — Anọ m n'ụlọ.
6. To ask about someone's dad: — Kedu maka nna gị?
7. To ask about someone's household: — Kedu maka mmadu niile nọ n'ụlọ?
8. To ask a friend if he or she remembers Uchenna: — I chetere Uchenna?
9. To ask if someone knows Chukwudi: — Ị maara Chukwudi?
10. To tell someone you do not know Chukwudi: — Amaghị m Chukwudi.
11. To ask if someone knows about an event: — Ị ma maka mmeme ahụ?
12. To tell someone 'you are about to go now': — Ka ọ dị oge ọzọ.
13. To tell someone, Yes, you can say: — Ee.
14. To ask for Chịọma's whereabout: — Ebee ka Chioma nọ?
15. To respond that you know Obinna: — Amataara m Obinna.
16. To ask if someone read about a story or news: — Ị gụrụ maka akụkọ ahụ?
17. To tell someone you have heard him or her: — Anụla m.
18. To tell someone you know a bit of something: — Obere.
19. To ask a friend if he or she heard about Obiọra: — Ị nụrụ maka Obiora?
20. To tell someone, No, you can say: — Mba.
21. To respond that another person is in Onitsha: — Ọ nọ Onitsha.

Glossary

Everyday phrases

 **Glossary**

1.	Ntakiri	A little bit
2.	Maka	About
3.	Na	And
4.	Zaa m	Answer me
5.	Nwee ndidi	Be patient
6.	Mechie ọnụ	Be quiet/Shut up
7.	Ma (mana)	But
8.	Bịa ebe a	Come here
9.	I nwere...?	Do you have….?
10.	I chọrọ enyemaka?	Do you need help?
11.	Ị na-asụ bekee?	Do you speak English?
12.	Nye m	Give me
13.	I riela nri?	Have u eaten?
14.	Ebe a	Here
15.	Ole?	How many?
16.	Ego ole?	How much?
17.	Ugboro ole?	How often?
18.	Kedu?	How?
19.	Mee ọsọ	Hurry up
20.	Ekwere m	I agree
21.	Abụ m	I am
22.	Ana m abịa	I am coming
23.	Ụra na-atụ m	I am feeling sleepy
24.	Agụụ na-agụ m	I am hungry
25.	Ekweghị m	I don't agree
26.	Anaghị m asụ bekee	I don't speak English
27.	Anaghị m asụ bekee nke ọma	I don't speak English very well
28.	Aghọtaghị m	I don't understand
29.	Achọghị m	I don't want
30.	Eriela m nri	I have eaten
31.	Enwere m...	I have…
32.	Aghọtara m	I understand

33.	Achọrọ m	I want
34.	Achọrọ m iri...	I want to eat...
35.	Achọrọ m ịnyụ amịrị	I want to pee
36.	Achọrọ m ịnyụ nsị	I want to poo
37.	Ejikerela m	I'm ready
38.	Biko, gbaghara m	Please, forgive me
39.	Oge o ruola?	Is it time?
40.	Ọ di mma	It is alright
41.	O siri ike	It is difficult
42.	Ọ di mma	It is good
43.	Oge eruola	It is time
44.	Mba (E e)	No
45.	Nsogbu adịghị	No problem
46.	Ma ọ bụ	Or
47.	Biko	Please
48.	Biko, bia	Please come
49.	Biko, kwugharịa ya	Please repeat
50.	kemgbe	Since
51.	Kemgbe ole?	Since when?
52.	Nọdụ ala	Sit down
53.	Jiri nwayoo kwube	Speak slowly
54.	Kwụrụ ọtọ	Stand up
55.	Imeela	Thank you
56.	Imeela	Thank you very much
57.	Nke ahụ	That
58.	Ebe ahụ	There
59.	Nke a	This
60.	Daalu	Well done!
61.	Gịnị mere?	What happened?
62.	Gịnị?	What?
63.	Ole mgbe?	When?
64.	Ebee?	Where?
65.	Onye?	Who?
66.	Maka gini?	Why?
67.	Ee	Yes
68.	Ị gbalịala	You tried.